EARLY DAYS

THE BEST OF LED ZEPPELIN VOLUME ONE

International MUSIC Publications

INTERNATIONAL MUSIC PUBLICATIONS LIMITED

ENGLAND: GRIFFIN HOUSE,
161 HAMMERSMITH ROAD, LONDON W6 8BS
GERMANY: MARSTALLSTR. 8. D-80539 MUNCHEN
DENMARK: DANMUSIK, VOGNMAGERGADE 7
DK 1120 KOBENHAVN

WARNER/CHAPPELL MUSIC

CANADA: 85 SCARSDALE ROAD, SUITE 101
DON MILLS, ONTARIO, M3B 2R2
SCANDINAVIA: P.O. BOX 533, VENDEVAGEN 85 B
S-182 15, DANDERYD, SWEDEN
AUSTRALIA: P.O. BOX 353
3 TALAVERA ROAD, NORTH RYDE N.S.W. 2113

Nuova CARISH S.p.A.

ITALY: NUOVA CARISCH SRL, VIA CAMPANIA 12
20098 SAN GIULIANO MILANESE, MILANO
FRANCE: CARISCH MUSICOM
25 RUE D'HAUTEVILLE, 75010 PARIS
SPAIN: NUEVA CARISCH ESPAÑA
MAGALLANES 25, 28015 MADRID
www.carisch.com

WARNER BROS. PUBLICATIONS
THE GLOBAL LEADER IN PRINT

USA: 15800 NW 48TH AVENUE, MIAMI, FL 33014

GOOD TIMES, BAD TIMES

Words & Music by
Jimmy Page, John Paul Jones and John Bonham

*Key signature indicates E Mixolydian mode.

*Let ring

*Let ring

*Let arpeggiated figures ring
throughout unless notated otherwise.

And now I've reached that age _ I've tried to do _

_(do ____) all those things _ the best I __ can. _ No

4

mat-ter how I try— I find my way in-to the same— old— jam.—

Chorus:

Good times, bad— times,— you know I've had— my share.—— Well, my

Let ring

Let ring *Rush tempo*

6

swore that she would be — all mine and love me 'till the end, — but

when I whis-pered in her ear — I lost an-oth-er friend. — Oh!

* Parenthesised notes played by Guitar 1 only

Chorus:

Good times, bad times, — you know I've had my share. — Well, my

Electric Guitar 1

Electric Guitar 2

Let ring   *Let ring*

wo-man left home for a brown-eyed man,____ but I still don't seem to care.____

(F#sus4)

Guitar Solo
With Fill 1 (8 times)

Fill 1

Even gliss.

Good times, bad times, __ you

know I've had my share. __ Well, my wo-man left home for a brown-eyed man, __ but I still don't seem to care. _____

Even gliss.

E5   N.C.   (D)   (A)

I don't care __ what the neigh - bors __ say, __

I'm gon - na love __ you each __ and ev - 'ry day. __

I know what it means to be a- lone, ___

I sure do wish I was at home. ___

Re - al - ize___ sweet_ babe ___ we ain't nev - er gon - na part. ___

Fade out

BABE I'M GONNA LEAVE YOU

Words & Music by
Anne Bredon, Jimmy Page and Robert Plant

Verse 1:

Coda 1

Fill 2
Slide Guitar (*with backwards echo*)

Tuning: ① =D

Dsus4/A   Dm/A   A5(addB)   Am7(no3rd)   Dsus4/A   Dm/A

Vocal ad lib. on D.S.

Am   Am7/G   D7/F♯

Ba - by, ___   C'mon,   Babe!

Acoustic Guitar *With Riff A(4 times) and With Fill 4 (16 times)*

Electric Guitar

Riff A

Fill 4

Pedal Steel Arr. For slide gtr.
Tuning: ① =D   *quick gliss*

I'm gon - na leave you girl, ____

oh, _____ Ba -

oh,   I___ can hear it cal - lin' me,___

With Riff B

D.S. 𝄋 *al Coda* ⊕

I said don't you hear it___ cal - lin'___ me the way___ it

Riff B

Pedal Steel *(Arranged for Slide Guitar)*

Tuning: ① =D

Coda 2

used to do.___

Acoustic Guitar Solo

I know, _____   I know, _____   I know I'm nev-er nev-

don't you hear it cal - lin' him?___

oh,___ wo - man,___

Fill 3

Even gliss.

32

(Alternate fingering)

That's when it's cal - lin' me,

It was real - ly

D7/F♯   F   E   D.S.%% al Coda ⊕

But now, _____   I've   got to   go a -

Even gliss.   *Even gliss.*

Coda 4   *Free time*

⊕   F

That's   when it's   cal - lin' me. ___

E7

F   E   *On cue*

I   said that's when it's   cal - lin' ____   me, _____ -   back ___ home. __

snap

DAZED AND CONFUSED

Words and Music by
Jimmy Page

soul   of   a   wo-man   was   cre-at-ed   be-low,_____   yeah._____

*Upstemmed part played through fuzztone with octave effect (8va higher).
This can also be recreated with a pitch transposer.

Verse 2:

You   hurt_____

___ and a-bused___ tell-in' all of your lies.___   Run 'round sweet ba - by, Lord,___ how they hyp-no-tize.__

Sweet lit-tle ba - by, I don't know where you been._   Gon - na love you ba - by, here I come a -

gain.

Guitars 1 and 2

Guitar 3

*Upstemmed part with 8va fuzz

Ev - 'ry

Verse 3:

day I work so hard— bring-in' home my hard-earned pay.   Try to love you ba-by, but you push me a-way.—

Don't know where you're go-in', I don't know just where you've been; sweet lit-tle ba-by, I want _ you a -

gain. _

Guitars 1 and 2

Guitar 3

ah, _____

ah, _____

14 12 10 12 10

+1

5

ah, _____ (ah) ___

Even gliss.

+1/2

9

7

ah, _____

div.

Even gliss.

14   10   12   7   10
14   10   12   7

14   (14)

* *Overdubbed fill. Tremelo with bow and wah wah.*

ah,   ah,   ah.

Continue tremelo with bow.

14   7   10   7
12   7   7   7

Oh,

Guitar tacet

oh _____ don't leave me so con - fused, _____

no!

Oh,

ba - by!____

Upstemmed part with 8va fuzz.

Been

dazed and con-fused for so long, it's not true,___ want-ed a wo-man nev-er bar-gained for you.___

Take it ea-sy ba-by, let them say what they will.__(Will your) tongue wag so much when I send you the

COMMUNICATION BREAKDOWN

Fast Rock ♩ = 174

Intro:

Words and Music by
Jimmy Page, John Paul Jones and John Bonham

Verse 1:

Hey, girl, ___ stop what you're do - in'. ___

Hey, ___ girl, ___ you'll

drive me to ru - in. ____ I don't ____ know ___ what it

is that I like ____ a - bout you ____ but I like it a lot. ____ Won't ___

Chorus:

to know   Hey, _____   babe, ___   I   wan - na

tell   you   that   I _____ love   you   so. _____

Chorus:

Com - mu - ni - ca - tion break - down, ___

it's al - ways the same. ___ I'm hav-ing a ner-

Com-mu - ni - ca - tion break - down,

Com - mu - ni - ca -

WHOLE LOTTA LOVE

Words and Music by
Jimmy Page, Robert Plant, John Paul Jones,
John Bonham and Willie Dixon

74

Fill 1

mf Slow, even gliss.
Slide guitar with backwards echo

Slow, even gliss.
Slide guitar with backwards echo

37

(Vocal, Guitar with Theremin, percussion effects)

Electric Guitar 2

You been___

Verse 3:

___ cool - in',___ and ba - by, I've been drool - in',_____

Guitar 1

all___ the good time___ ba - by, I been___ mis - us - in'.___

WHAT IS AND WHAT SHOULD NEVER BE

Words and Music by
Jimmy Page and Robert Plant

Verse 2:

mor - row,   oh, what fun it   all ___ would be. ___

Then what's to stop us pret-ty ba - by ___   but what is and

what should ___ nev-er be. ___   I catch the wind ___ see us spin, sail a-way, leave to day, ___

way up high, in the sky Hey, oh then the wind ___ won't blow,   you real-ly should-n't go.   It

Verse 3:

So if you wake up with the sun-rise and all your dreams are

still as new.___ And hap-pi-ness is what you need so bad,___

Girl, the ans-wer lies ___ with you ___ yeah. I

Catch the wind, see us spin, sail a-way, leave to-day, way up high in the sky___ Hey, Oh, but the

Hey _____ Ho _____ Well, the

wind _ won't blow, and you real-ly should-n't go, well it on - ly goes to show. Oh _ oh oh

Catch the wind, _ we're gon-na see you spin, _ we're gon-na sail _____ leave to-day _____

Ah, du du du, mm ba, ba, mm du _ oh

IMMIGRANT SONG

Words and Music by
Jimmy Page and Robert Plant

* Note: All chord names reflect composite guitar harmonies.
** With amplifier vibrato set to 16th note pulse.

Verse 1:

come from the land of the ice and snow, from the mid - night sun where the hot springs ___ flow. ___

Continue amplifier vibrato

F#(addG#)

___ Ham-mer of ___ the gods, will drive our ships to new ___

Guitar 1

Guitar 3 *(Guitar 2 tacet)*

** *Muted scratch/strum-roughly parallels the bass part.*

Return 16th note amplifier vibrato

C

Our on - ly goal will be the west - ern — shore. —

* Overdub

(Intro:)

F♯(addG♯)

Ah, _____

mf

F#(addG#)

Ah.

Verse 2:

A5   E5

We come from the land of the ice and snow, from the

Return 16th note amplifier vibrato with Guitar 2.

Asus9   F#(addG#)

mid-night sun where the hot springs ___ flow. ___ How   soft ___ your fields _____ so green.   Can

Guitar 1

Guitar 2

Guitar 3

Return muted scratch/stum part.

whis - per   tales ___ of   gore. ___   Of

Guitar 3   *(Guitar 2 tacet)*

F♯(addG♯)   F♯5   A5   E5

how   we   calmed...   the   tides   of   war. __   We   are __   your

Guitar 1

Guitar 2

Guitar 3

Return 16th note amplifier vibrato.

E5   A5   F♯(addG♯)

ov - er   Lords. _____

*Additional Guitar in unison with
original (treble pick-up with distortion.)*

F♯(addG♯)

now you'd bet-ter stop, ___ and re-build all ___ your ru-ins. For

So

* div.

* Upstemmed part on beats 3&4: additional guitar fill.

peace and trust can win the day, de - spite of all your los - ing.

SINCE I'VE BEEN LOVING YOU

Words and Music by
Jimmy Page, Robert Plant and John Paul Jones

*Les Paul: volume is varied throughout (approximate: neck = 10, bridge = 7).

**Chords implied by the organ bass pedals.

***Chords stated or implied by the organ. Passing chords in parenthesis. This Fm7 can also be thought of as Ab/F. This chord voicing approach is used on the organ throughout the song.

****Both pickups: neck = 10, bridge = 7.

107

*Bridge (lead) pickup only = 10

**Both pickups: neck = 10, bridge = 7.

*Add fuzztone.

**Interior strings are muted with left hand.

Fuzztone out.

**Position hand at first fret.*

***Re-position hand at third fret.*

tell,   let me tell you I real-ly did the   best I   could. __

I've been, I've been work-ing from   sev - en,

ah,   to e - lev - en ev' - ry night, __ I   said it kind - a makes my

life a drag,   drag, drag, drag,   Lord, _____

yeah _____ that ain't right __ now, now.

Since _____ I've been lov-in' you, __   I'm a-bout to lose __   my wor-ried

mind.   Watch out!

Guitar II:

*Add fuzztone.
**Third string muted with fretting hand. Open second string occurs later
in the song and may be a guitar error, but is notated for accuracy.
***Fifth string muted with fretting hand. See suggested fingering. Fuzztone out.
****Bridge pickup: 10, with medium fuzz.

Bridge:
Guitar Solo

*Add fuzztone.
**Downstrums only through measure eleven.

114

Fuzztone out.

Verse 3:

Said I've been cry - in, yeah.___   Oh my tears they fell like rain,___

don't you hear,___   don't you hear them fal - ling, .

don't you hear,___   don't you hear them   fal - ling?___

Guitar 1

Guitar 2 out

*Downstrums. Add fuzztone.

Notes and lyrics in parentheses are whispered here.

*Fuzztone out.
**Slide down and up repeatedly.

BLACK DOG

Words and Music by
Jimmy Page, Robert Plant and John Paul Jones

*Guitar 1 (Right channel) is in downstems and Guitar 2 (Left channel) is in upstems.

**This pitch is from a tape effect and not playable. See Performance Notes.

***Enter on drummer's cue.

****Guitar 2 enters and sustains its A5 chord into Verse 2, whereas
Guitar 1 plays it's A5 chord again on the downbeat of Verse 2.

Guitar 1 is faded out in the first measure. (Simile for all verses)

Unh, nh child, ___ way you shake that thing, ___ gon-na
Heh, hey ba - by when you walk walk that way, ___ watch

make you burn, ___ gon - na make you sting. ___
heart-ache drip, ___ can't make keep a - way. ___

Guitars 1 and 2 **

**Guitar 2 joins Guitar 1 through Verse 3.*

*The Guitar 2 part omits the upper note of each power chord throughout the Chorus

Guitar 1 begins a slide up to A, while Guitar 2 repeats A5.

F *Verse 4:*

I got-ta roll, can't stand still,— got-ta flame-in' heart,— can't get my— fill.

Guitar 3 out

Guitar 2 out

**Guitar 1 fades out and Guitar 2 sustains.*

*Guitar 1 is faded out in the second measure.

**Guitar 1 is faded out in the second measure.

***Feedback harmonic

I *Chorus 2:*

ah._____ Hey hey ba - by, oh____ ba - by,

*Crescendo on upper note in vocal(e).
**Hammer on between thumb and second finger.

pret - ty ba - by, dar - lin' can't you do me now?_

***Although these are the proper chords, various notes are emphasized each time they're strummed.
****The note E is played here by the Bass guitar only, throughout Choruses 2 and 3.

while you do me now.＿

Did-n't

J *Verse 6:*

take too long___ 'fore I found out___ what peo-ple mean___ by down and out.___

K *Verse 7:*

Spent my mon-ey, took my car,___ start-ed tell-in' her friends___ she gon-na

Guitar 1 fades out in measure 3.

*Guitar 1 fades out in measure 2.

N *Chorus 1:*

The Guitar 1 and 2 parts have been combined.
The Guitar 2 part omits the upper note of each power chord throughout the Chorus.

All I ask — for, all I pray, — stead - y load - ed wom - an gon -

*Guitar 1 slides into A5 and fades out in measure 2, Guitar 2 sustains.

na come my — way.

A5

P *Verse 10:*

A5

Need a wom - an, gon - na hold my hand___ will tell me no___ lies,___ make me a

Guitar 1 fades out in measure 2.

N.C.

hap - py man. _____

G *Bridge:*

*Guitar 3 fades out in measure 1, Guitar 1 in measure 2, and Guitar 2 sustains throughout.

**Crescendo on upper note in vocal, decrescendo on the lower note.
***Guitar 3 is recorded through a Leslie amplifier (rotating speakers), and on a separate track with a standard amplifier.

R

Chorus 3(Guitar solo):

*Standard amplifier from here on, no Leslie.
**Volume in mix is much lower.

137

Guitar 3

Leslie amp returns, standard amp out.

Begin Guitar 4 figure 2
Guitar 4**

End Guitar 4 figure 2

Push it, ba - by, push it, ba - by, push it, ba - by,

push it, ba - by, push it, ba - by, push it, babe

babe.

**Guitar 1, figure 1 mixed lower to make room for Guitar 4, figure 1. (Right Channel)*
Continue with Guitar 2, figure 1.

Continue figure 1, Guitars 1 and 2 and continue figure 2, Guitar 4, 6 times till fade.

ROCK AND ROLL

Words and Music by
Jimmy Page, Robert Plant, John Paul Jones
and John Bonham

*All chords in parentheses are implied.

*Mute the sixth string with the fret hand thumb after bending G.

been a long time since I did the stroll._____

Guitars I and II *

Ooh, let me get it back, let me get it back, let me get it

back, ba - by where I____ come from.____

It's

*From here on Guitar I and II are written together. Guitars I and II continue to maintain their tones
(Guitar I: heavy distortion/ambient, Guitar II: light distortion/direct.)

*Let the sixth string ring.

Guitar 1

Guitar 2

Guitar 3

Oh, _____ Its been a long time, been a

long time, been a long lone-ly, lone-ly, lone-ly, lone-ly, lone-ly

time. Aww, _____

Guitar 1

Guitar 2

Guitar 3

D **Bridge:**
(A7)

Oh, _____ Oh. _____

Guitar 1 and 2

Guitar 3

(D7) (A7)

(E7) (A7)

E *Verse (Guitar Solo):*
(A7)

(D7)

Oh _____ it seems so long _ since we

walked in the moon - light._____ Mak- ing vows,— that

just can't work right. ha - ha - yeah,— Op- en your arms, op- en your arms,   op - en   your arms. ___

Ba - by let love ___ come

(A7)

runn - ing in.

Yes. ___

E5

It's been a long   time,   been a   long   time,   been a long

D5

lone - ly,   lone - ly,   lone - ly,   lone - ly,   lone - ly,

yeah, —— hey, yeah, —— hey,

Ooh, yeah   Ooh, yeah_   Ooh, yeah   Ooh, yeah._   (It's)

Guitar 3 out

been a long   time,   been a   long   time, been a long   lone - ly,   lone - ly, lone - ly, lone - ly, lone - ly

Drum Outro: *(free tempo)*

time.

On Cue
A7

Original tempo

Guitar 2

Guitarist gives cue out of solo.

THE BATTLE OF EVERMORE

Words and Music by
Jimmy Page and Robert Plant

Mythical Folk Ballad freely ♩ = 144
With a strong half-time feel

* *Composite of Mandolins 1 and 2.* ***Arranged for Guitar with capo at X. All notes in TAB at X are notated as open.*
To be played one octave higher until **G**

Tape echo. Include these beats to simulate the recording when performing without echo/delay.

158

* *Chord names are a composite of the Mandolin & Guitar parts.*

** *Six and Twelve string Guitars.*

*This part is optional and omitted from here on.

* Female voice replaces male voice.
**Distant Male Chorus. (Right Channel)

From here on the Guitar arrangement is notated without the tape echo rhythms.

* *Female voice replaces male voice.*

P Choral Verse:

At last, _____ the sun ___ is shin - in' the ___

clouds ___ of blue ___ roll by. _____

With flames ___ from the dra - gon of dark - ness the

sun - light it blinds his eyes. _____

* *Long crescendo next 24 bars to forte.*

*The suggested strum is intended to emphasize the descending line of the mandolin within a counterrhythm. When playing with the recording, be careful with the tempo.

** Play fingerstyle. The low notes are strummed with the thumb or pick and the high notes are plucked with the fingers.

* Due to fingering difficulties, all notes on ④ and ⑤ are optional.

now oh now oh. Oh now, oh now, oh now. Bring it!

T *Coda:*

A5sus9/13   G(addA)   A5sus9/13   C(addA)

Bring it!   Bring it!   Bring it!   Bring it! ____ Bring it!

WHEN THE LEVEE BREAKS

Words and Music by
Jimmy Page, Robert Plant, John Paul Jones,
John Bonham and Memphis Minnie

*Bb major or an F Blues harp.

**Open F tuning: ④ = C, ③ = F, ② = A, ① = C. ⑥ and ⑤ aren't used in the recording.
12 string octave and unison strings aren't notated. Slide is worn on fourth finger to be ready for A .

***Implied.

Regular time feel

185

Guitars 1 appear with phase shifting until the following verse.
*Worn on fourth finger.

*Guitar 1 appears with phase shifting for the rest of the song.

**These chord names are implied by the guitar only and do not reflect the bass part.

***A Les Paul in standard tuning through a fuzztone and played with a slide.

make ya' feel bad__ when ya' tryin' ta' find your way home ya' don't know__ which way (to) go,-

——— if ya' go-in down south they got no work to do if ya'

*Final note of phrase from Guitar 2.

With Guitar 2 Rhythm Figure 1
With ad lib. variations

194

*Arpeggiate.
**Harmonica first time only.

Cry-in' won't help_ ya' pray-in' won't do_ ya' no good, no,—

cry-in'won't help_ ya', pray-in' won't do— ya' no good. (Ah)when the

lev-ee breaks,— ma-ma you got_ to move.———————— Ah, ooo,—— ooo.

*Blues Harp first time only.
**Guitars 1 & 2 are combined.

*Harmonica with backwards echo enters and continues intermittently for the remainder of the song.

Guitar 1 gradually panned to the left.
**Guitar 1 gradually panned right.*

*Slide Guitar (backwards echo track only).
**Panned left and right every four measures.

Go - in' down,_____ go - in'

down now,_____ go - in' down,_____ go - in' down now,_____ go - in'

now. Ah, woo, ah, woo.

*Backwards echo track only from here on.
The notation and techniques are an approximation of the original recording.

STAIRWAY TO HEAVEN

Words and Music by
Jimmy Page and Robert Plant

Epical Ballad: Chamber Folk to Heavy Rock
Slowly ♩ = 72 (gradual accellerando)

Capo at VII using a cutaway guitar with easy access to the 22nd fret. All notes in TAB at VII are open strings.

**The open first string is not played here, but rings sympathetically.*

***A gradual decrescendo continues for the next four measures to allow for the entrance of the recorders.*

*The actual pitch of this note(e) is one octave higher

Ooo, _____ and she's buy - ing a stair - way_ (to)

heav - (en). There's a sign on the wall_ but she wants to be sure,_ 'cause you

*The Acoustic Guitar is multi-tracked from here on.
**With a pick.

*Suggested strum

feel - ing I get___ when I look to the west,___ and my spir - it is cry-ing for leav-

Let ring

Rhythm Figure 1

ing. In my thoughts I have seen___ rings of smoke through the trees___ and the

Let ring

Suggested fingering.
**T=Thumb on ⑥

voic - es of those who stand look - ing.

Acoustic 6 string

Electric 12 string 1

Electric 12 string 2 (R&LC)   *Rhythm Figure 2*

Ooo, _____ it makes me won - der.

pp cresc.

mp

End Rhythm Figure 2   *Gtr. 2 Tacet*

* *Strings ④ and ② are muted while ③ and ① are open.*

**Separate track – Sustain and fade over.

***Separate track.

216

*Doubled with an Electric 6 string (Telecaster?) from here on.

**( ) Acoustic Guitar track only.

the pip - er's call - ing you__ to join__ him. Dear la - dy can you hear the wind-

blow, and did you__ know,__ your stair- way lies on the whis - 'prin' wind.__

Oh.__

Acoustic Guitar (L.C.)

cresc.

Electric 12 string (R&LC)

cresc.

**The tempo is resumed by a cue from the guitarist.*

*Notes in parenthesis are upper notes of quieter background track.

I **Bridge:***(Guitar Solo)*

*Electric 6 string Guitar 1 (R & LC)

Electric 12 string Guitars 1&2(R&LC)

*1958 Telecaster through a Fender Suproamp?

** punch in from a separate track

*Played with a glass or metal slide.

224

226

Verse: With Rhythm Figure 3 with ad lib variations

♩ = 102

And as we wind on down the road, our shad-ows tal-ler than our soul,

*Palm muting is alternated (off then on) as in this two measure phrase from here on, but not notated.

Rhythm Figure 3
Electric 12 string Guitar 3 (RC)

*Mute strings with fret hand at current chord position.

there walks a la - dy we all know

who shines white light and wants to show how ev - ry thing still turns to

*Right and left channels from here on.

gold. _____ And if you list-en ver-y hard, _____

the tune will come to you at last, when all are one and one is all.

*Pan to center.
**Doubling ends.

Lead vocal in downstems, distorted chorus track in upstems.

*Pre-bent from here on

VSO (variable speed/pitch oscilator) 1/2 step glide.

234

Fade out

buy - ing a stair - way___ to heav - en.___

Oscillate guitar volume knob rhythmically.

Notation and Tablature Explained

Open C chord

Scale of E major

High E (1st) string
B (2nd) string
G (3rd) string
D (4th) string
A (5th) string
Low E (6th) string

Bent Notes

The note fretted is always shown first. Variations in pitch achieved by string bending are enclosed within this symbol ⌐ ⌐. If you aren't sure how far to bend the string, playing the notes indicated without bending gives a guide to the pitches to aim for. The following examples cover the most common string bending techniques:

Example 1
Play the D, bend up one tone (two half-steps) to E.

Example 2
Play the D, bend up one tone to E then release bend to sound D. Only the first note is picked.

Example 3
Fast bend: Play the D, then bend up one tone to E as quickly as possible.

Example 4
Pre-bend: fret the D, bend up one tone to E, then pick.

Example 5
Play the A and D together, then bend the B-string up one tone to sound B.

Example 6
Play the D and F♯ together, then bend the G-string up one tone to E, and the B-string up a semitone to G.

Additional guitaristic techniques have been notated as follows:

Tremolo Bar
Alter pitch using tremolo bar. Where possible, the pitch to aim for is shown.
a) Play the G; use the bar to drop the pitch to E.
b) Play the open G; use the bar to 'divebomb', i.e. drop the pitch as far as possible.

Mutes
a) Right hand mute
Mute strings by resting the right hand on the strings just above the bridge.
b) Left hand mute
Damp the strings by releasing left hand pressure just after the notes sound.
c) Unpitched mute
Damp the strings with the left hand to produce a percussive sound.

Hammer on and Pull off
Play first note, sound next note by 'hammering on', the next by 'pulling off'. Only the first note is picked.

Glissando
a) Play first note, sound next note by sliding up string. Only the first note is picked.
b) As above, but pick second note.

Natural Harmonics
Touch the string over the fret marked, and pick to produce a bell-like tone. The small notes show the resultant pitch, where necessary.

Slide Guitar
a) Play using slide.
b) Play without slide.

Artificial Harmonics
Fret the lowest note, touch string over fret indicated by diamond notehead and pick. Small notes show the resultant pitch.

Vibrato
Apply vibrato, by 'shaking' note or with tremolo bar. As vibrato is so much a matter of personal taste and technique, it is indicated only where essential.

Pinch Harmonics
Fret the note as usual, but 'pinch' or 'squeeze' the string with the picking hand to produce a harmonic overtone. Small notes show the resultant pitch.

Pick Scratch
Scrape the pick down the strings – this works best on the wound strings.

Microtones
A downwards arrow means the written pitch is lowered by less than a semitone; an upwards arrow raises the written pitch.

Repeated Chords
To make rhythm guitar parts easier to read the tablature numbers may be omitted when a chord is repeated. The example shows a C major chord played naturally, r/h muted, l/h muted and as an unpitched mute respectively.

Special Tunings
Non-standard tunings are shown as 'tuning boxes'. Each box represents one guitar string, the leftmost box corresponding to the lowest pitched string. The symbol '•' in a box means the pitch of the corresponding string is not altered. A note within a box means the string must be re-tuned as stated. For tablature readers, numbers appear in the boxes. The numbers represent the number of half-steps the string must be tuned up or down. The tablature relates to an instrument tuned as stated.

Tune the low E (6th) string down one tone (two half-steps) to D.

Chord naming
The following chord naming convention has been used:

Where there is no appropriate chord box, for example when the music consists of a repeated figure (or riff) the tonal base is indicated in parenthesis: [C]

Where it was not possible to transcribe a passage, the symbol ∿ appears.

Indications sur la notation musicale et les tablatures

Accord de Do majeur ouvert   Gamme de Mi majeur

- Mi aigu: 1ère corde
- Si: 2e corde
- Sol: 3e corde
- Ré: 4e corde
- La: 5e corde
- Mi grave: 6e corde

Bending

La note correspondant à la case sur laquelle on pose le doigt est toujours indiquée en premier. Les variations de hauteur sont obtenues en poussant sur la corde et sont indiquées par le symbole: ⌐ ¬. En cas de doute sur la hauteur à atteindre, le fait de jouer les notes indiquées sans pousser sur la corde permet de trouver ensuite la bonne hauteur. Les examples suivants démontrent les techniques de bending les plus courantes.

Exemple 1
Jouez la note Ré et poussez la corde d'un ton (deux demi-tons) pour atteindre le Mi.

Exemple 4
'Pre-bend': posez le doigt sur la case de Ré, poussez d'un ton pour atteindre le Mi avant de jouer la note.

Exemple 2
Jouez le Ré, poussez sur la corde pour atteindre le Mi un ton plus haut, relâchez ensuite pour revenir au Ré. Seule la première note est jouée avec le médiator.

Exemple 5
Jouez La et Ré simultanément; poussez ensuite sur la corde de Si pour atteindre la note Si.

Exemple 3
'Fast Bend': jouez le Ré et poussez le plus rapidement possible pour atteindre le Mi.

Exemple 6
Jouez Ré et Fa# simultanément; poussez la corde de Sol d'un ton vers le Mi, et la corde de Si d'un demi-ton vers le Sol.

D'autres techniques de guitare sont notées de la façon suivante:

Emploi du levier de vibrato
Modifiez la hauteur du son avec le levier de vibrato. Lorsque c'est possible, la note à atteindre est indiquée.
a) Jouez le Sol et appuyez sur le levier de vibrato pour atteindre le Mi.
b) Jouez un Sol à vide et détendez le plus possible la corde avec le levier de vibrato pour rendre un effect de 'bombe qui tombe' (divebomb).

Mutes (étouffements)
a) Mute de la main droite
Etouffez en posant la main droite sur les cordes, au-dessus du chevalet.
b) Mute de la main gauche
Relâchez la pression sur la corde juste après avoir joué la note.
c) Mute sans hauteur définie
Etouffez les cordes avec la main gauche pour obtenir un son de percussion.

Hammer On et Pull Off
Jouez la première note; frappez la corde sur la touche (Hammer On) pour obtenir la seconde note, et relâchez la seconde note en tirant sur la corde (Pull Off) pour obtenir la troisième note. Seule la première note est donc jouée avec le médiator.

Glissando
a) Jouez la première note avec le médiator, faites sonner la seconde note en ne faisant que glisser le doigt sur la corde.
b) Comme ci-dessus, mais en attaquant également la seconde note avec le médiator.

238

Harmoniques naturelles
Posez le doigt sur la corde au dessus de la barrette indiquée, et jouez avec le médiator pour obtenir un son cristallin. Le cas échéant, une petite note indique la hauteur du son que l'on doit obtenir.

Guitare Slide
a) Note jouée avec le slide.
b) Note jouée sans le slide.

Harmoniques artificielles
Posez le doigt (main gauche) sur la note la plus basse: effleurez la corde avec l'index de la main droite au-dessus de la barrette indiquée par la note en forme de losange, tout en actionnant le médiator. La petite note indique la hauteur du son que l'on doit obtenir.

Effet de Vibrato
Jouez le vibrato soit avec le doigt sur la corde (main gauche), soit avec le levier de vibrato. Comme le vibrato est une affaire de technique et de goût personnels, il n'est indiqué que quand cela est vraiment nécessaire.

Harmoniques pincées
Appuyez le doigt sur la corde de la façon habituelle, mais utilisez conjointement le médiator et l'index de la main droite de façon á obtenir une harmonique aiguë. Les petites notes indiquent la hauteur du son que l'on doit obtenir.

Scratch
Faites glisser le médiator du haut en bas de la corde. Le meilleur effet est obtenu avec des cordes filetées.

Quarts de ton
Une flèche dirigée vers le bas indique que la note est baissée d'un quart-de-ton. Une flèche dirigée vers le haut indique que la note est haussée d'un quart-de-ton.

Accords répétés
Pour faciliter la lecture des parties de guitare rythmique, les chiffres de tablature sont omis quand l'accord est répété. L'example montre successivement un accord de Do majeur joué de façon normale, un 'mute' de la main droite, un 'mute' de la main gauche et un 'mute' sans hauteur définie.

Accordages spéciaux
Les accordages non-standards sont indiqués par six cases, chacune représentant une corde (de gauche à droite), de la plus grave à la plus aiguë. Un tiret indique que la tension de la corde correspondante ne doit pas être altérée. Un nom de note indique la nouvelle note à obtenir. Pour les tablatures, les chiffres indiqués dans les cases représentent le nombre de demi-tons dont ou doit désaccorder la corde, vers le haut ou vers le bas.

Accordez la corde de Mi grave un ton plus haut de façon à obtenir un Fa#, et la corde de La deux tons plus haut de façon à obtenir un Do#.

Noms des accords

Lorsqu'aucun nom d'accord précis n'est applicable, par exemple quand la musique consiste en une figure répétée (riff), le centre tonal est indiqué entre parenthèses: [C]

Lorsqu'un passage n'a pas pu être transcrit, le symbole ~ apparait.

Hinweise zu Notation und Tabulatur

Offener C - Dur - Akkord   E - Dur - Tonleiter

Hohe E-Saite (1.)
H-Saite (2.)
G-Saite (3.)
D-Saite (4.)
A-Saite (5.)
Tiefe E-Saite (6.)

Gezogene Noten

Die gegriffene Note wird immer zuerst angegeben. Das Zeichen ⌐ ¬ zeigt eine Veränderung der Tonhöhe an, die durch das Ziehen der Saiten erreicht wird. Falls Du nicht sicher bist, wie weit die Saite gezogen werden soll, spiele die entsprechenden Töne zunächst ohne Ziehen; so kannst Du Dich an der Tonhöhe orientieren. Die folgenden Beispiele geben die gebräuchlichsten Techniken zum Ziehen wieder:

Beispiel 1
Spiele das D und ziehe dann um einen Ton (zwei Halbtonschritte) höher zum E.

Beispiel 4
Im Voraus gezogen: Greife das D, ziehe um einen Ton höher zum E und schlage erst dann die Saite an.

Beispiel 2
Spiele das D, ziehe um einen Ton hoch zum E und dann wieder zurück, so daß D erklingt. Dabei wird nur die erste Note angeschlagen.

Beispiel 5
Spiele A und D gleichzeitig und ziehe dann die H-Saite um einen Ton nach oben, so daß H erklingt.

Beispiel 3
Schnelles Ziehen: Spiele das D und ziehe dann so schnell Du kannst um einen Ton höher zum E.

Beispiel 6
Spiele D und Fis gleichzeitig; ziehe dann die G-Saite um einen Ton nach oben zum E und die H-Saite um einen Halbtonschritt nach oben zum G.

Zusätzliche Spieltechniken für Gitarre wurden folgendermaßen notiert:

Tremolo
Verändere die Tonhöhe mit dem Tremolo-Hebel. Wenn es möglich ist, wird die angestrebte Tonhöhe angezeigt.
a) Spiele G; nutze den Takt, um zum E abzusteigen.
b) Spiele die leere G-Saite; nutze den Takt, um so weit wie möglich abzusteigen.

Dämpfen
a) Mit der rechten Hand
Dämpfe die Saiten, indem Du die rechte Hand einfach oberhalb der Brücke auf die Saiten legst.
b) Mit der linken Hand
Dämpfe die Saiten, indem Du den Druck der linken Hand löst, kurz nachdem die Töne erklingen.
c) Ohne bestimmte Tonhöhe
Dämpfe die Saiten mit der linken Hand; so erzielst Du einen 'geschlagenen' Sound.

Hammer on und Pull off
Spiele die erste Note; die zweite erklingt durch 'Hammering on', die dritte durch 'Pulling off'. Dabei wird nur die erste Note angeschlagen.

Glissando
a) Spiele die erste Note; die zweite erklingt durch Hochrutschen des Fingers auf der Saite. Nur die erste Note wird angeschlagen.
b) Wie oben, aber die zweite Note wird angeschlagen.

Natürliches Flageolett
Berühre die Saite über dem angegebenen Bund; wenn Du jetzt anschlägst, entsteht ein glockenähnlicher Ton. Wo es nötig ist, zeigen kleine Notenköpfe die entstandene Note an.

Slide Guitar
a) Spiele mit Rutschen des Fingers.
b) Spiele ohne Rutschen.

Künstliches Flageolett
Greife die unterste Note, berühre die Saite über dem durch Rauten angegebenen Bund und schlage dann den Ton an. Die kleinen Notenköpfe zeigen wieder die entstandene Note an.

Vibrato
Beim Vibrato läßt Du die Note für die Dauer eines Tons durch Druckvariation oder Tremolo-Hebel 'beben'. Da es jedoch eine Frage des persönlichen Geschmacks ist, wird Vibrato nur dort angegeben, wo es unerläßlich ist.

Gezupftes Flageolett
Greife die Note ganz normal, aber drücke die Saite mit der zupfenden Hand so, daß ein harmonischer Oberton entsteht. Kleine Notenköpfe zeigen den entstandenen Ton an.

Pick Scratch
Fahre mit dem Plektrum nach unten über die Saiten – das klappt am besten bei umsponnenen Saiten.

Vierteltöne
Ein nach unten gerichteter Pfeil bedeutet, daß die notierte Tonhöhe um einen Viertelton erniedrigt wird; ein nach oben gerichteter Pfeil bedeutet, daß die notierte Tonhöhe um einen Viertelton erhöht wird.

Akkordwiederholung
Um die Stimmen für Rhythmus-Gitarre leichter lesbar zu machen, werden die Tabulaturziffern weggelassen, wenn ein Akkord wiederholt werden soll. Unser Beispiel zeigt einen C - Dur - Akkord normal gespielt, rechts gedämpft, links gedämpft und ohne Tonhöhe.

Besondere Stimmung
Falls eine Stimmung verlangt wird, die vom Standard abweicht, wird sie in Kästchen angegeben. Jedes Kästchen steht für eine Saite, das erste links außen entspricht der tiefsten Saite. Wenn die Tonhöhe einer Saite nicht verändert werden soll, enthält das Kästchen einen Punkt. Steht eine Note im Kästchen, muß die Saite wie angegeben umgestimmt werden. In der Tabulaturschrift stehen stattdessen Ziffern im entsprechenden Kästchen: Sie geben die Zahl der Halbtonschritte an, um die eine Saite höher oder tiefer gestimmt werden soll.

Stimme die tiefe E-Saite (6.) um einen Ganzton (zwei Halbtonschritte) höher auf Fis und die A-Saite (5.) um zwei Ganztöne (vier Halbtonschritte) höher auf Cis.

Akkordbezeichnung
Die folgenden Akkordbezeichnungen wurden verwendet.

Wenn kein eigenes Akkordsymbol angegeben ist, z.B. bei Wiederholung einer musikalischen Figur (bzw. Riff), steht die Harmoniebezeichnung in Klammern: [C]

Das Symbol ∼ steht jeweils dort, wo es nicht möglich war, einen Abschnitt zu übertragen.

Spiegazione della notazione e dell'intavolatura

Accordo di Do aperto
(in prima posizione)

Scala di Mi maggiore

Mi acuto: la corda
Si: 2a corda
Sol: 3a corda
Re: 4a corda
La: 5a corda
Mi basso: 6a corda

Bending

La prima nota scritta è sempre quella tastata normalmente. Le alterazioni di altezza da realizzare con la trazione laterale della corda (bending) interessano le note comprese sotto al segno: ⌐ ⌐ ⌐. Se siete incerti sull'entità dell'innalzamento di tono da raggiungere, suonate le note indicate tastando normalmente la corda. Gli esempi seguenti mostrano le tecniche più comunemente impiegate nella maggior parte dei casi che possono presentarsi.

Esempio 1
Suonate il Re e innalzate di un tono (due mezzi toni) a Mi.

Esempio 4
'Pre-Bend': tastate il Re, tirate alzando di un tono a Mi e poi suonate.

Esempio 2
Suonate il Re, tirate alzando di un tono a Mi e rilasciate tornando a Re. Va suonata solo la prima nota.

Esempio 5
Suonate simultaneamente La e Si quindi tirate la 2a corda per innalzare il suono a Si.

Esempio 3
'Bend Veloce': suonate il Re e quindi alzate di un tono a Mi il più velocemente possibile.

Esempio 6
Suonate simultaneamente Re e Fa# quindi tirate la 3a corda alzando il suono di un tono a Mi, e la 2a corda di mezzo tono, alzando il suono a Sol.

Negli esempi seguenti sono illustrate altre tecniche chitarristiche:

Barra del tremolo
Alterate l'altezza del suono mediante la barra del tremolo. Dove possibile l'altezza da raggiungere è indicata.
a) Suonate il Sol e abbassate il suono fino a Mi mediante la barra.
b) Suonate il Sol a vuoto e scendete quanto più possibile.

Smorzato
a) Smorzato con la destra
Smorzare le corde con il palmo della mano destra in prossimità del ponticello.
b) Smorzato con la sinistra
Smorzare le corde allentando la pressione delle dita subito dopo aver prodotto i suoni.
c) Pizzicato
Premere leggermente le corde in modo che non producano note ma soltanto un effetto percussivo.

Legature ascendenti e discendenti
Suonate la prima nota e ricavate la seconda percuotendo la corda con il dito contro la barretta; per la terza nota tirate la corda con il medesimo dito. Soltano la prima nota va suonata.

Glissando
a) Suonate la prima nota e ricavare la seconda facendo scivolare il dito lungo la corda. Va pizzicata solo la prima nota.
b) Come sopra, ma pizzicando anche la seconda nota.

Armonici naturali

Toccate leggermente la corda sulla barretta indicata e pizzicate col plettro per produrre un suono di campana. Le notine indicano il suono risultante, dove occorra.

a) b)

Slide Chitarra

a) Suonare con slide.
b) Suonare senza slide.

Armonici artificiali

Tastate la nota più bassa, toccate leggermente la corda sulla barretta relativa alla nota romboidale e pizzicate con il plettro. Le notine indicano il suono risultante.

Vibrato

Effettuate il vibrato facendo oscillare il dito che preme la corda oppure con la barra del tremolo. Poichè il vibrato è un fatto di gusto personale, viene indicato solo dove è essenziale.

Armonici pizzicati

Tastate normalmente la nota ma pizzicate la corda con la mano destra per ricavare l'armonico sopracuto. Le notine indicano l'altezza del suono risultante.

Suono graffiato

Fate scorrere il bordo del plettro lungo la corda. L'effetto è maggiore sulle corde fasciate.

Microintervalli

Una freccia diretta verso il basso significa che il suono scritto va abbassato di un intervallo inferiore al semitono; una freccia diretta verso l'alto innalza il suono scritto.

Accordi ripetuti

Per facilitare la lettura, possono venire omessi i numeri nell'intavolatura di un accordo ripetuto. L'esempio mostra un accordi di Do maggiore suonato normalmente, smorzato con la destra, smorzato con la sinistra e pizzicato (muto).

Accordature Speciali

Le accordature diverse da quella normale sono indicate in speciali 'gabbie di accordatura'. Ogni gabbia rappresenta una corda di chitarra; all'estremità sinistra corrisponde la corda più bassa. Il simbolo '•' in una gabbia sta ad indicare che l'intonazione della corda corrispondente è quella normale. Una nota nella gabbia indica che l'intonazione di quella corda va modificata portandola all'altezza indicata. Per coloro che leggono l'intavolatura, dei numeri posti nelle gabbie stanno ad indicare di quanti semitoni deve salire o scendere l'intonazione della corda. L'intavolatura è da considerarsi relativa ad uno strumento accordato come indicato nelle gabbie.

Accordate la corda del Mi basso (6a) un tono sopra (due semitoni) a Fa#. Accordate la corda del La basso (5a) due toni sopra (quatro semitoni) a Do#.

Indicazione degli accordi

E' stata impiegata la seguente nomenclatura convenzionale degli accordi.

C   Cm   C5   Csus4   Csus$\frac{4}{2}$ C(b5)   Cdim   Caug   C6   Cm6   Cmaj7   C7   C7#5   C7b5   Cm7   Cm7b5   Cdim7   Cmaj9   C9   Cm9   C7b9   C7#9   Cadd9   C/Bb

Quando non compare la griglia appropriata di un accordo, ad esempio, quando la musica consiste nella ripetizione di una stessa figura (riff), la base tonale è indicata fra parentesi: [C]

Dove non è stato possibile trascivere il passaggio, compare il segno ~ .

Printed in England
The Panda Group · Haverhill · Suffolk · 7/00